10667596

DEATH VALLEY

A Day in the Desert

BY

NANCY SMILER LEVINSON

ILLUSTRATED BY

DIANE DAWSON HEARN

Holiday House / NEW YORK

PUBLIC LIBRARY, PLAINFIELD, NJ

Thanks are due to Death Valley National Park for cooperation, and
to Roger Brandt, Park Ranger; Pat Compton, Visitor Services;
and Dick Anderson, Environmental Specialist, for their special assistance.
James Murakami, Research Associate, Atmospheric Science Department,
University of California, Los Angeles, was also helpful
in the preparation of this book.

Text copyright © 2001 by Nancy Smiler Levinson
Illustrations copyright © 2001 by Diane Dawson Hearn
All Rights Reserved
Printed in the United States of America
www.holidayhouse.com
First Edition
Reading Level: 2.9

Library of Congress Cataloging-in-Publication Data
Levinson, Nancy Smiler.
Death Valley: a day in the desert / by Nancy Smiler Levinson;
illustrated by Diane Dawson Hearn.—1st ed.
p. cm.
Summary: Describes the desert habitat of Death Valley and
the plants and animals that live there.
ISBN 0-8234-1566-X (hc.)
1. Natural history—Death Valley (Calif. and Nev.)—Juvenile literature.
2. Desert ecology—Death Valley (Calif. and Nev.)—Juvenile literature.
[1. Natural History—Death Valley (Calif. and Nev.) 2. Desert ecology—
Death Valley (Calif. and Nev.)
3. Ecology—Death Valley (Calif. and Nev.)]
I. Hearn, Diane Dawson, ill. II. Title.
QH104.5.D4 L48 2001
508.794'87—dc21
00-023305

For Eve Bunting,
who led the way
N. S. L.

With thanks
to Jonathan Kingston
D. D. H.

kit fox
scorpion

There is a desert
in California.
It is called
Death Valley.

A desert is dry land
and dry air.

The Arctic and Antarctic are deserts, too. They are cold, polar deserts.

Most deserts are hot.
Death Valley is one of the
hottest of all.
How hot is it?
In summer,
the temperature can rise to
125 degrees!

red-tailed hawk

desert spiny lizard

The ground gets even hotter.
It gets up to 200 degrees.
That would melt the rubber
on a pair of sneakers.
That's hot!

What can you see in Death Valley?
There are mountains and rocks,
salt flats and sand.
There are bushes and cactus plants,
but no trees are growing.
And there is bright sunlight.

mouse
beehive cactus

Hardly any rain falls in Death Valley.
Mountains keep out moist air
and low rain clouds.

The air is so dry,
the soil crumbles
and turns to sand.

The wind blows
the sand into big hills.
They are called sand dunes.
It also carves rocks
into many shapes.

sidewinder

Plants and wildflowers
live in Death Valley.
Only tough plants can survive.

The creosote bush holds water
in its leaves, stems, and roots.
It can hold the water for months.

Mormon cricket
gopher snake

A barrel cactus can save a life.
If a thirsty traveler gets lost,
he can cut off the cactus top.
Then he can drink the pulpy
juice inside.

Small animals live in Death Valley.
Pocket mice and kangaroo rats
live in tunnels deep in the ground.

big
free-tailed
bats
desert cottontail

At night the desert air cools fast.
That is when animals come out
to search for food.

kit fox

wild burros
red-spotted toad
killdeer

Death Valley mammals,
reptiles, and birds
find water in creeks
and in springs under the ground.

Where does the water come from?
Once or twice a year in Death Valley,
the sky turns dark.
The clouds burst.

Rain rushes down in a wall of water.
It rains for only an hour or two.
That is enough to keep the desert
alive.

Common Death Valley Animals and Plants

bobcat

big
free-tailed bat

kangaroo rat

MAMMALS

ground squirrel

coyote

AMPHIBIANS

red-spotted
toad

ARACHNIDS

scorpion

desert tarantula

BIRDS

roadrunner

great horned owl

raven

REPTILES

chuckwalla

sidewinder

desert tortoise

PLANTS

Joshua tree

Mojave yucca

More about Death Valley

—Death Valley National Park is part of the Mojave Desert.

—The highest air temperature recorded there was 134 degrees.

—Rainfall averages less than two inches a year. Most rain evaporates into the air.

—The temperature averages 65 degrees on winter days. At night it drops to about 40 degrees.

—Hundreds of species of mammals, reptiles, and birds live there.

—The lowest elevation in the Western hemisphere is in Death Valley. It is called Badwater and lies 282 feet below sea level.

—Nearly one million people visit Death Valley every year.

80025 75540